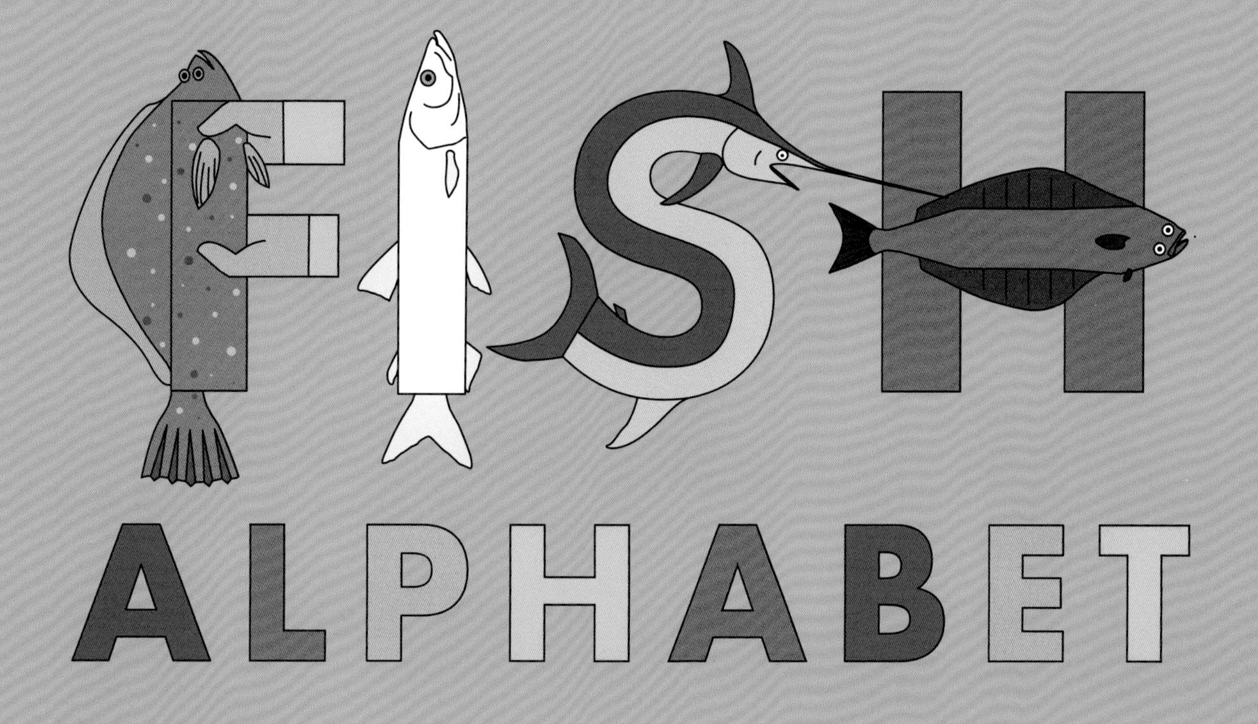

Words by Robin Feiner

Aa

A is for Greater **A**mberjack. Easy on the eye but not necessarily on the plate, this legend can be found swimming around the reefs of the Gulf Coast and the Caribbean. Just be ready to dive deep for an epic angle with this spirited sea dweller.

Bb

B is for Bass.

Arguably the most popular freshwater fish in North America, for millions of anglers it's all about the bass. From largemouth and smallmouth black bass to spotted and striped varieties, these lunkers are targets for tournament entrants and casual casters alike. Save a spot on the wall for your next big catch.

C is for Catfish.
Only a true pro can get
one of these tasty treats
off the hook without getting
cut by its legendary razor-
sharp whiskers. From blue
to channel to flathead, you
can find catfish in just about
every region of the US.
They're a freshwater
favorite for frying up.

Dd

D is for Dorado.
You might know this speedy fish by its more common name of mahi-mahi, which means 'very strong' in Hawaiian. Any saltwater angler can tell you the name fits. This west coast wonder's gorgeous, electric color scheme is only matched by its delicious flavor.

Ee

E is for Escolar.
Swimming around Hawaii, escolar has been a local legend for decades. While there's no harm in catching what's often called walu or oilfish, eating escolar is another thing entirely. Before digging in, read up on the controversy surrounding it.

F is for Flounder.
Flounder is a form of flatfish with a wide, round, flat body and both eyes on the same side of its head. These bottom-dwellers are a good target if you're new to sea fishing, as they're easier to catch than some other salty sea species.

Gg

G is for Grouper.
There's no shortage of this fish in North American waters. You'll find great groups of grouper at varying depths off the Gulf of Mexico. Outlast its legendary initial dash and avoid a snapped line, and you'll pull a delicious catch.

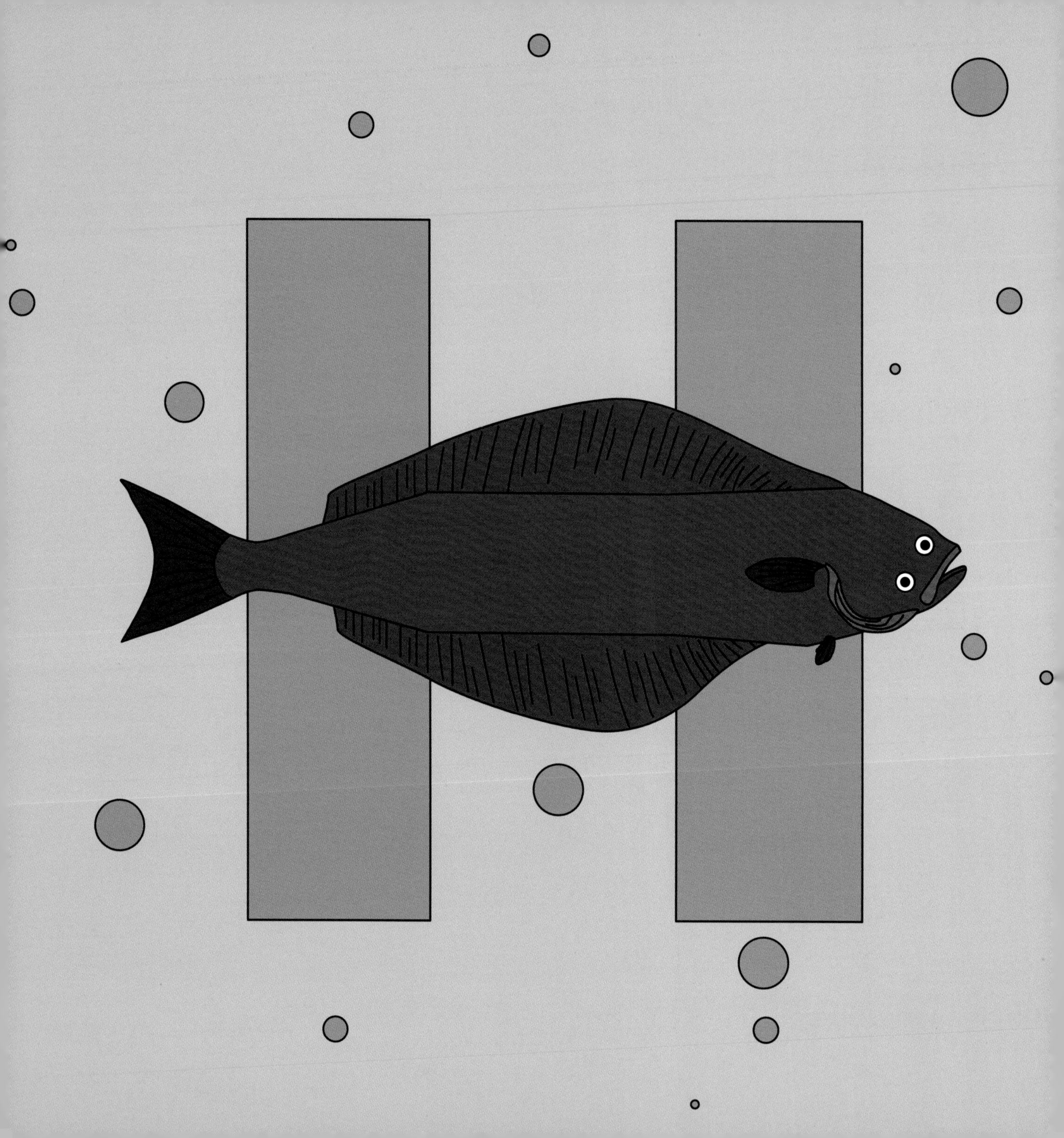

H is for Halibut.
Species of this fish really get around, migrating throughout the Atlantic and Pacific, with the larger ones generally found off the east coast. The holy halibut name was inspired by its popularity on Sundays in England. It still fries up quite nicely no matter where you are.

Ii

I is for Inconnu.
This Canadian monster is a fierce fighter and legendary leaper. Also called the Eskimo tarpon, it's a whitefish that loves to chow down on smaller species, so tie up a lure that looks like a tiny fish to get inconnu eyes wide. And don't forget to bundle up.

Jj

J is for Jack.
A battling jack will put up one of the finest fishing fights in the sea. It's not the most prestigious catch, nor the tastiest. But casting your line into a school of these jacks is a surefire way to have some fun. And that's a fact, Jack.

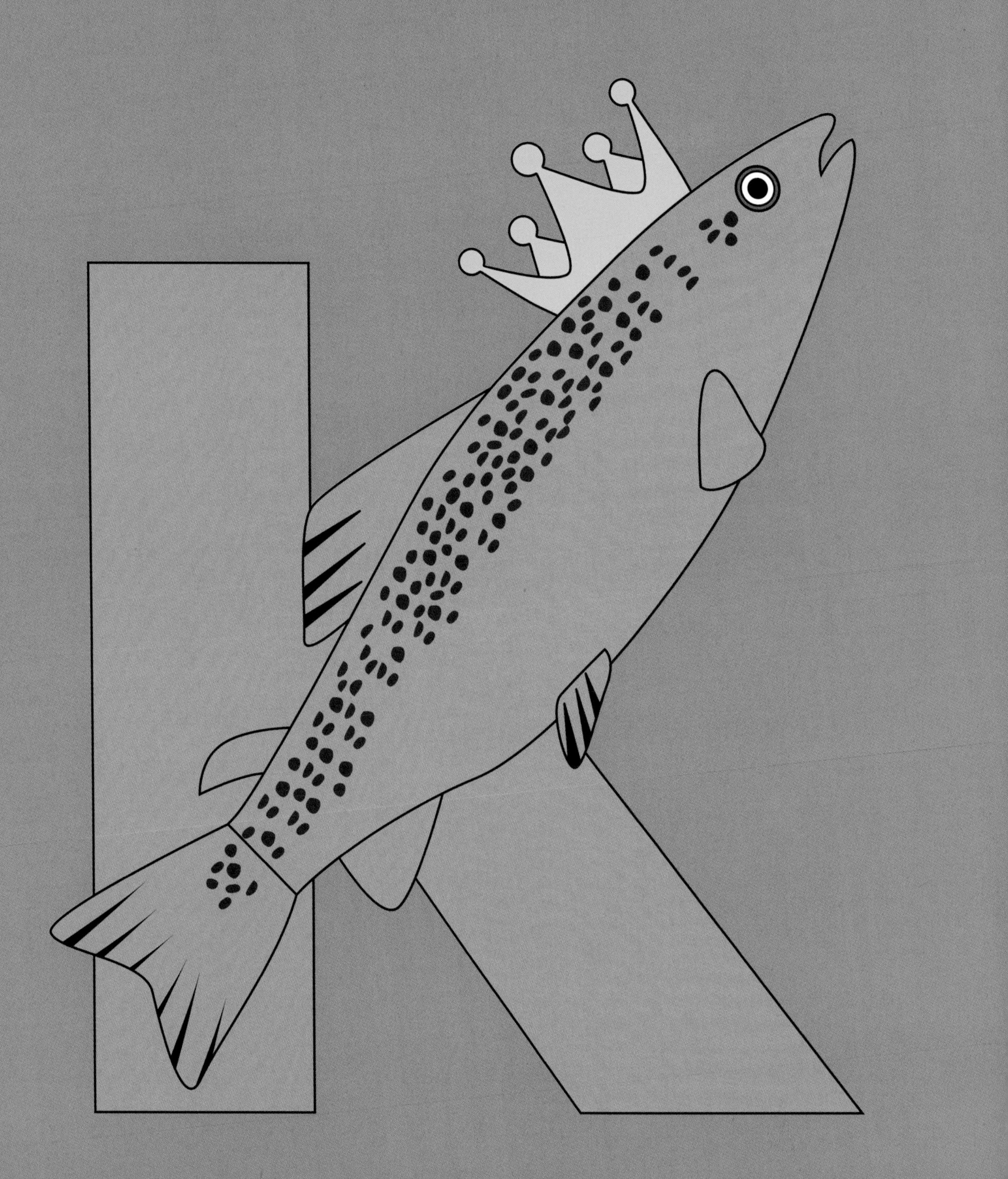

Kk

K is for King Salmon. All hail this legend. Every fisher knows bigger is better, and the king, or chinook, proves it. Its delicious, deep flavor is your reward for finding one of these giants in the rivers of the Pacific Northwest or Alaska.

L is for Lingcod.
True casters know that the lingcod isn't actually a cod, but a greenling. They won't win any beauty contests with their large heads and darker-colored, spotted bodies. But they still look great on your stringer before a clean and cook after a session on the water.

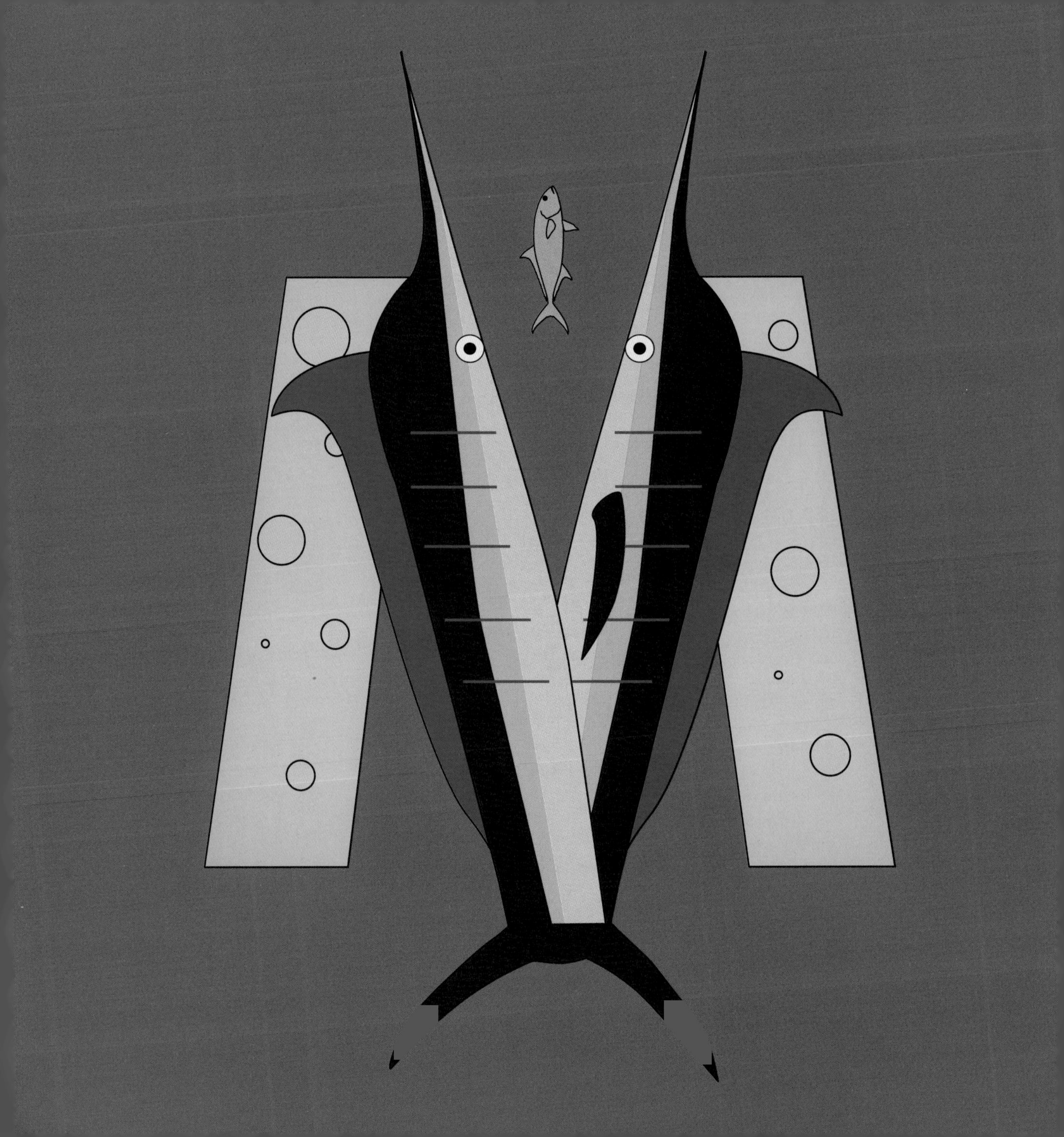

Mm

M is for **M**arlin.
While white and black are nice, nothing tops the majestic blue marlin. The pinnacle of sport fishing, these beauties are found swimming around in wide-open, warmer seas. Seeing one in full flight on the end of your line is the stuff angling dreams are made of.

Nn

N is for Northern Pike.
This toothy king of the north
is nothing to mess with.
A northern pike loves the
cold almost as much as it loves
eating. And experienced ice
fishers know the fight doesn't
end after pulling this legend
from the water. Mind those
infamous sharp jags under
the gills when cleaning.

O is for Opah.
Count yourself lucky if you land a gorgeous, round opah. Their beautiful, bright bodies match the tropical ocean waters they live in. Nicknamed the moonfish, the opah doesn't stay in one place for long, making this disc-shaped species quite a catch for California casters.

Pp

P is for Perch.
Let's give a hand to the prince of panfish, which are catches that generally fit in a frying pan. Some species of perch, such as the plentiful yellow perch, can be a great target for little anglers, as they're not too big or strong.

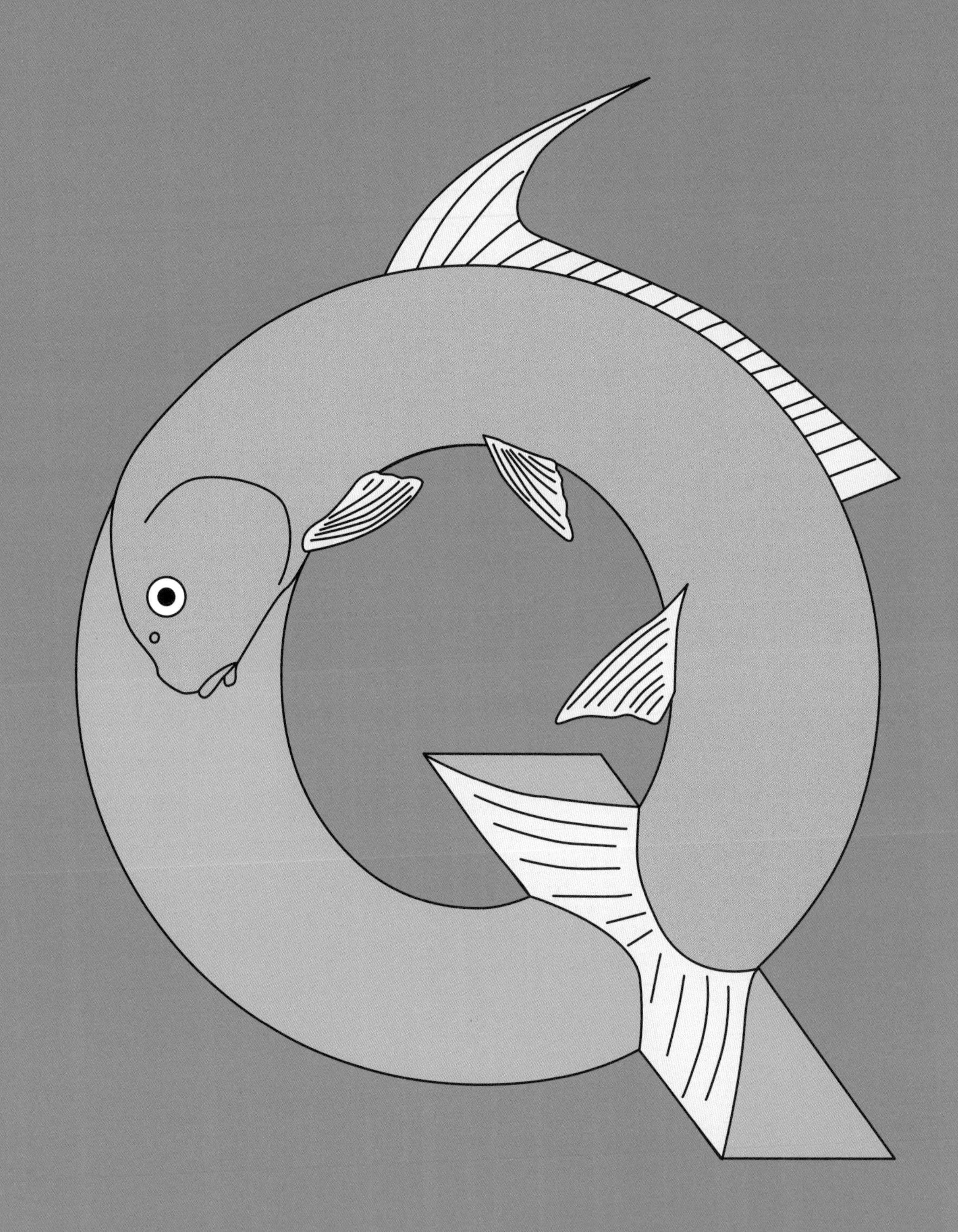

Qq

Q is for Quillback Carpsucker. The best thing you'll get from catching this freshwater fish is bragging rights, as it's more about the test than the taste. Not particularly eye-catching either, this legendarily slow, picky eater isn't known for taking the bait. Strike quickly when chances arise.

R is for Red Snapper.
The arrival of red snapper season can feel like its own holiday. There's nothing quite like heading to your favorite honey hole and trolling the depths to land one of these delicious whitefish. Just don't get frustrated when they keep stealing your bait.

Ss

S is for **S**wordfish.
Your weapon of choice better be strong when trying to catch this beast. You need to be really dedicated with the reel – whether it be electric or manual – if you're going to pull a swordfish over the side of your boat. It's perhaps the toughest fighter in the sea.

Tt

T is for Rainbow Trout. There's nothing like bagging your daily limit of these legends. Chuck on the waders, find your preferred river or stream spot, pop a night-crawler on the hook, and get ready to cast when that opening siren tells you fishing season has returned.

Uu

U is for Unicorn Leatherjacket. Also called the unicorn filefish, you won't find horns or rain-bow tails here. In fact, tales of landing one close to home are so rare that this elusive fish might be fantasy anyway. Cast a line off California, Mexico, or Florida to find the truth for yourself.

Vv

V is for Dolly Varden.
Good golly, the Dolly Varden is one fine-looking fish. Like trout but with brighter colors that look gorgeous mounted on the wall, your best bet is to head to Alaska to find one. Use a small spinner or spoon that resembles baby salmon – a preferred Dolly Varden snack.

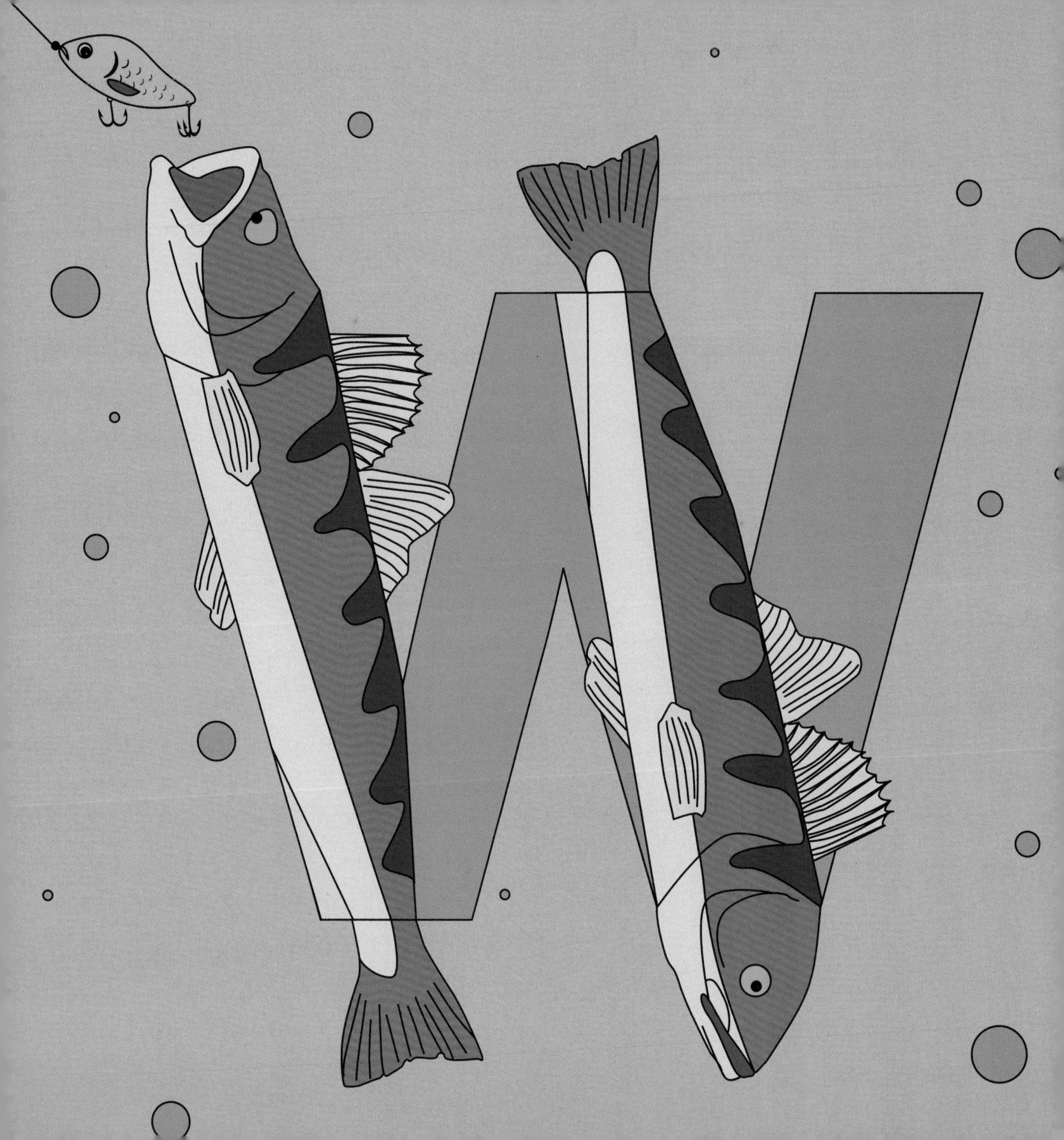

Ww

W is for **W**alleye Pike.
Caught throughout the US,
the walleye pike is a fishing
favorite around the country.
Outfitting your tackle box and
vest with lures, heading out
in the low light and filling up
your livewell – it's the perfect
way to start or end your day.

X is for Xantic Sargo. Its alias of California sargo will tell you where to find this legend. You might not have to go far to track one down, either, as the xantic sargo can be caught off the famous piers and shores of the Golden State.

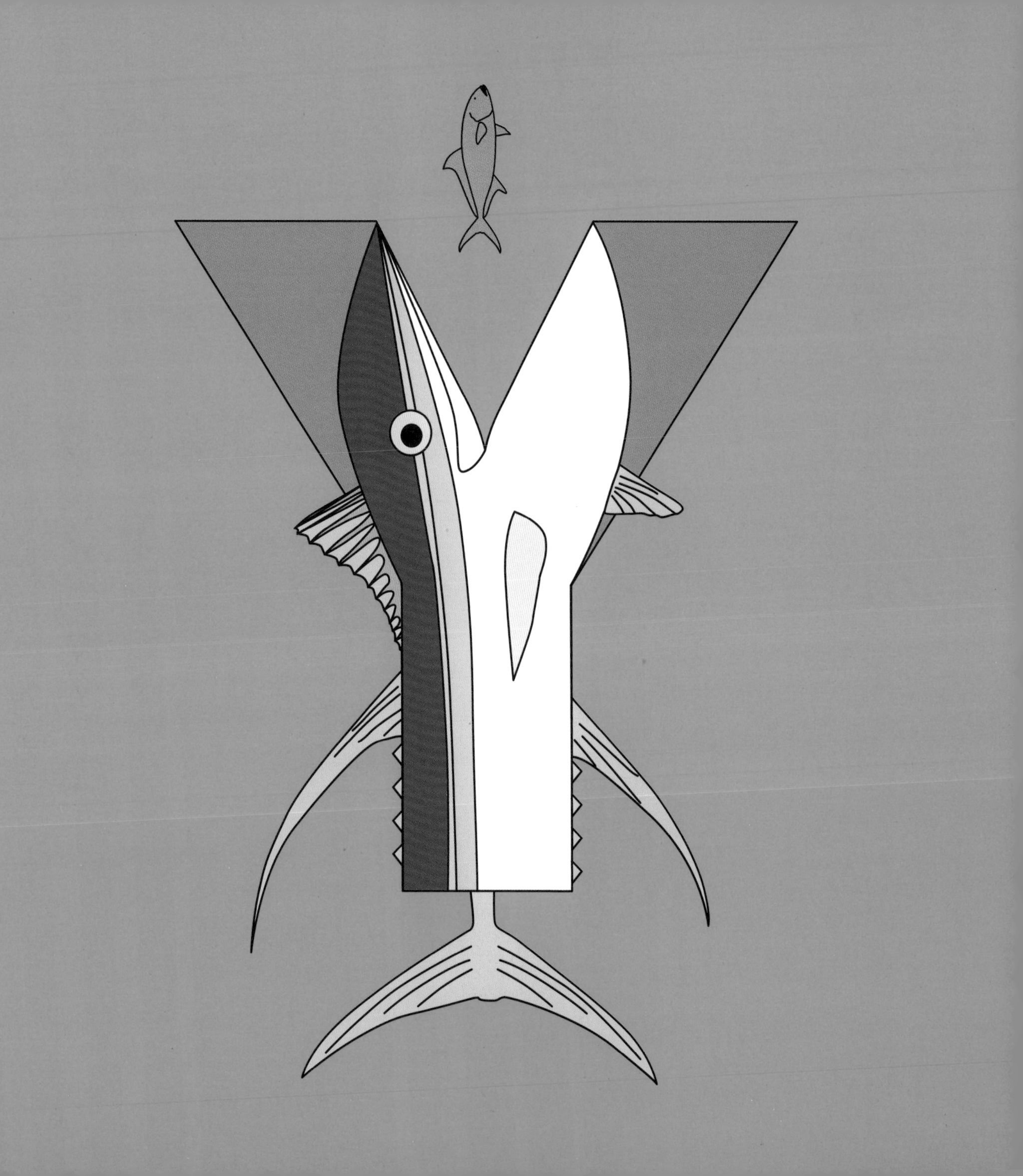

Yy

Y is for Yellowfin Tuna.
One of the most alluring fish on the planet, the yellowfin is a true trophy tuna. Keep a lookout for these beauties surface feeding in tropical and subtropical waters. Routinely weighing hundreds of pounds, you have to be a real rod-and-reel wizard to earn this catch.

Zz

Z is for Zander.
Pack your rods and reels and head to North Dakota to find this legend in the US. There, in select lakes, you'll find this European catch. To this day it fools many a fisher, as it looks – and tastes – very similar to a walleye.

The ever-expanding legendary library

EXPLORE THESE LEGENDARY ALPHABETS & MORE AT WWW.ALPHABETLEGENDS.COM

FISH ALPHABET
www.alphabetlegends.com

Published by Alphabet Legends Pty Ltd in 2022
Created by Beck Feiner

Printed and bound in China.

9780645487046

ALPHABET LEGENDS